Beef Cattle Auction Guide for Farmers and Ranchers

Complete Details on How to Plan and Hold Your Own Beef Cattle Auction

Introduction

"Don't be afraid to take a big step if one is indicated. You can't cross a chasm in two small jumps."
David Lloyd George

Even though I've been around cattle all my life, auctions have always seemed like mysterious ceremonies that could be performed only by specially anointed people (that is, the auctioneers). In fact, auctions were so shrouded in secrecy that it seemed arrogant for me to even think of holding an auction of my own. In 1984, though, I decided to do it anyway. It didn't take long for me to find out just how little I knew about livestock sales. Even though I hired someone to manage the sale, I didn't even know the right questions to ask.

I've held many sales since then, and each time I've learned a little more about how the process works. But I still remember how it felt, that first time around, to know almost nothing at all. Hopefully, this book will give you an advantage I didn't have. In fact, I'm hoping that even if you're a seasoned professional, you'll find new information here.

I considered extending the scope of this book to include the sale of other livestock such as horses, sheep, goats, and pigs. In the end, I decided against it because my expertise is in cattle. Nevertheless, I suspect that no matter what kind of animal you raise, you'll find this volume useful.

Thank you for taking the time to purchase and read this book. If you like what you read (Or even if you don't), please write and tell me. I look forward to hearing from you.

2016 Update

This book is for anyone interested in learning how to hold their own Beef Cattle Auction and anyone just wanting to learn more about the inner workings of Beef Cattle Auctions.

If you are searching for a new marketing method for your cattle and looking for more information about "How to Hold Your Own Cattle Auction" on your farm or ranch, please read on.

Just wanting to know more about the inner workings of a cattle auction, please read on.

In today's high tech world we don't have to think of just local buyers when it comes to a Beef Cattle Auction.

Today's landscape for an auction has changed to an almost unlimited audience of prospective buyers through the use of the Internet, Cell Phones and other Electronic Devices. We can all agree that more prospective buyers should make for a better sale.

A good Sales Manager or Auctioneer should have a well-developed marketing plan and know how to determine the needed manpower to pull off a successful sale. You as the seller, together with your sale manager can apply cost figures to this plan to estimate the financial need to help determine the resources to hold your own cattle auction.

The fundamental reason behind cattle auctions from the seller's point of view is to get maximum value for their cattle. On the other hand, the buyers view or reason for buying at an auction is because they are looking for the best deal possible. On the surface it sounds like one of them is sure to be disappointed. However, there is something some of us refer to as dollar cost averaging. A good sale manager will have a good handle on this theory and how to apply it in a manner that makes a good sale experience for both buyers and seller. The secret here is to let your sale manager and auctioneer to work for you in the manner he knows best. Do not try to second guess his ability or tie his hands in any way.

Please enjoy the rest of this book.

Table of Contents

Chapter One: Why Hold an On-Farm Cattle Sale?
"It's kind of fun to do the impossible."
Walt Disney

Chapter Two: Creating Your "Cast of Thousands"
"The way to get things done is not to mind who gets the credit for doing them." Benjamin Jowett

Chapter Three: Details, Details
"Obstacles are those frightful things you see when you take your eyes off your goal." Henry Ford

Chapter Four: Preparing for the Sale
"There are no shortcuts to any place worth going." Beverly Sills

Chapter Five: The Day of the Sale
"The problem is not that there are problems. The problem is expecting otherwise and thinking that having problems is a problem." Theodore Rubin

Conclusion
"Don't judge each day by the harvest you reap but by the seeds you plant." Robert Louis Stephenson

About the Author
"I still find each day too short for all the thoughts I want to think, all the walks I want to take, all the books I want to read, and all the friends I want to see." John Burroughs

Chapter One
Why Hold an On-Farm Cattle Sale?

"It's kind of fun to do the impossible."
Walt Disney

Many ranchers never consider holding an on-farm sale. After all, as this book makes clear, holding a cattle sale is a major undertaking, requiring you to manage many logistical details. Wouldn't it be easier just to sell by private treaty?

Sure, it might be easier in the short run. However, it is actually more expensive to sell by private treaty than by sale. Take advertising, for example. When you advertise for private treaty sales, your advertising dollars target individual ranchers looking to make small purchases of just a few head of cattle. This is particularly true where your advertisement features a few specific animals. In contrast, when you hold a sale, the same number of dollars will sell many cattle and bring in many buyers to see your stock.

If you think only big ranches can hold sales, think again. In some ways, smaller ranches have the advantage. With lower overhead and advertising costs, they can afford to sell for less.

Furthermore, the sale itself is a wonderful marketing tool for your ranch and your breed. You will have the opportunity to present your ranch and your stock at its very best, not only to buyers and potential buyers, but to everyone involved in the sale itself. Remember, everyone who comes into contact with your ranch is a potential marketer. The auctioneer, the sales manager, the cowboys, the veterinarian -- any of them may refer buyers to you in the future. And each successive sale will bring more and more referrals who have heard about your past sales.

Holding a sale isn't without its disadvantages, though, and it's not for everyone. For one thing, holding a sale is expensive. In addition to advertising costs, you will incur costs for personnel, equipment, and perhaps even food for your guests. It doesn't make sense to hold a sale for unregistered cattle, registered cattle of lower breeding quality, or animals destined for the feedlot. It's not cost- effective if you have just a few head to sell, either. Therefore, the costs of an on-farm sale are best suited for a large number of high quality -- and high-priced -- breeding stock.

Second, holding a sale also requires a large one-time cash outlay. While your long- term marketing costs are lower with a sale than with private treaty sales, you can at least pay them a little at a time. In an auction, though, your costs are incurred – and have to be paid – all at once. Although most of the costs of an auction will be paid out of your proceeds, some costs must be paid up front. And as soon as the sale is over, you'll have some sizeable bills to pay. If you're not prepared to pay them when they're due, then a sale may not be for you.

Third, holding a sale takes a lot of planning, done well in advance. You've got to line up the auctioneer and all the other people who will be involved in the sale; you've got to arrange for equipment rentals, worry over logistics, choose which animals to sell, and print the catalog. If you aren't in a position to plan several months in advance, then holding a sale is probably unwise.

Finally, it takes a few sales before you start to see the maximum benefit from them. True, your first few sales will bring people who have seen your advertising. But once you've established yourself, word-of-mouth will bring in even more buyers. In fact, if you have a sale every year, always at about the same time, buyers may come to look forward to, and even count on, your ranch's sale to build their herd. After all, why spend weeks scouring market bulletins and trade magazines for seed stock if you can do it in one day at a really good sale?

So, is an on-farm sale for you? It might be, if you can answer yes to the following questions:

- Do I have high-quality, registered breeding stock?

- Do I have enough cattle to sell?

- Can I plan the sale months in advance?
- Can I spend the money required to put on the sale?
- Do I have sufficient space and facilities to hold a sale?
- Will I be able to accommodate parking, unloading, and loading?
- Can I hold sales on a regular basis?

Chapter Two
Creating Your "Cast of Thousands"

"The way to get things done is not to mind who gets the credit for doing them." Benjamin Jowett

If you're reading this book, you're probably already familiar with sales of registered livestock. A sale held on your own ranch is not much different. The sale will be publicized in the appropriate magazines and bulletins, and a catalog will be available for potential buyers. Your auction will be well- organized and efficient. The auctioneer, sales manager, ring men, and other personnel will work together to see that the sale moves along quickly. When an animal is sold, a ticket writer will make a record of the sale. A bill of sale will be written, and after the sale, the buyer will pay for his lots. The staff will settle accounts with the buyers, health certificates will be issued, and cattle will be loaded out. The auction may be a day-long affair with food, drinks, and lots of social interaction between the buyers and the rancher's staff.

What you may not know, however, is how much work goes on behind the scenes. It takes many people to manage a sale efficiently. If it's done right, the sale will go so smoothly that the buyers may never realize how much time and effort it takes. The key to success is in the planning. A lot of that planning has to do with hiring people to make your job as easy as possible.

Auctioneer or Sales Manager? Once you've decided to hold a sale, you first need to decide whether or not to hire a sales manager. The sales manager's job is to coordinate the auction so you don't have to. He can recommend auctioneers, and once you choose an auctioneer, he can work with the auctioneer to line up ring men, cowboys, and other personnel. Your sales manager can also make sure the appropriate equipment is available, handle the logistics of parking and transportation, and make sure that the proceeds of the sale are properly accounted for. In short, the sales manager's job is to make sure your sale goes smoothly, allowing you to relax and enjoy the festivities. In that sense, a sales manager is very much like a wedding planner!

If you don't want to hire someone, you can act as your own sales manager. This means that you will coordinate the proceedings. You will be responsible for every detail of the sale, from hiring personnel to loading the cattle onto the trucks, unless you delegate the task to someone else. If you forget to plan for any detail, you may end up having to do it alone.

Generally, it's a good idea to hire an experienced sales manager for your first two or three sales, unless you have lots of experience and even more confidence. Let your sales manager teach you the ropes, and then perhaps you will feel confident enough to manage the sale yourself. By then, you will probably have a relationship with an auctioneer you like, and managing the sale will be much easier.

Whether or not you hire a sales manager, it's a good idea to know as much as you can about the other players that will help you run the auction.

Finding an Auctioneer

The auctioneer, of course, is the person who will call the sale of each animal. It's his job to get the highest possible price for your stock. A really good auctioneer can not only call the sales, but give you good advice before the sale about stock selection, pricing for specific animals, the order of the sale, and marketing, among other things. Moreover, the auctioneer will act as your representative before the public. A professional, efficient, ethical auctioneer will attract buyers now and in the future. A bad auctioneer will cost you money long after the sale is over. For that reason, it's important to choose the right person.

The best auctioneer is someone who is experienced not only with cattle generally, but with your breed and with the local market. Such a person may be difficult to find if you raise one of the rarer breeds, but it's important to get as close as you can to this ideal.

Your sales manager, if you hire one, can probably provide recommendations. If not, or if you are acting as the sales manager, you can find prospective auctioneers by contacting your breed association and other ranchers. It's also a good idea to attend as many auctions as you can, particularly for your breed, so that you can get to know the auctioneers.

When you have your list of prospective auctioneers narrowed down to a reasonable few, contact them and ask some specific questions. **Among them:**

- How does he calculate his fee? Is there a minimum amount? What does his fee include? How should he be paid?
- Does he just sell the animals, or can he provide a "turnkey" operation working in conjunction with the sales manager?
- What experience does he have with your breed and with the local market?
- Does he have his own sound equipment? Will he be recording the sale? (Keeping an audio or video record of the sale can

help you resolve disputes quickly later on).

- Does he have any special recommendations for selecting the animals you offer for sale?
- Does he have any ideas or recommendations for finding bidders, or for (or against) pre- selling your animals?
  - What is his procedure with floor- priced animals? For example, how will you know when an animal has not sold?
  - What recommendations does he have for the sale order? For example, does he like to sell the most valuable animals first?
- What personnel does he furnish? For example, does he provide his own ring men or ticket writers?
- Does he recommend that you accept cattle on consignment?
- What are his usual procedures for bidder registration?
- Does he issue bidder numbers?

(He may use names if he knows the buyers, but using numbers can prevent misunderstandings later)

- Does he have someone who can talk about the animals, or do other tasks of a sales manager?
- Does he have preferences about other personnel, such as cowboys?
- Will he prepare the bills of sale? If so, does he have the appropriate forms?
- Does he have any recommendations or preferred procedures for handling last minute catalog changes or substitutions?

The Ring Men

Besides the auctioneer and the sales manager, there are a number of people that can either make or break your sale. The most important of these, by far, is the ring man.

The ring man's job, to put it bluntly, is to "work the audience" to encourage higher bidding. He comments on the animals, urges the audience members to bid higher, and helps make sure bids are communicated to the auctioneer.

In addition, the ring man communicates with the auctioneer – sometimes in ways that buyers can't see – to make sure the sale is successful. There are usually at least three ring men in the audience.

A good ring man can liven things up considerably, adding entertainment to the proceedings. This alone can bring people in, once word gets around. And some of the folks who came just to watch will end up buying.

It is absolutely essential that the ring men and the auctioneer work well together – so important, in fact, that the auctioneer should choose his own ring men. A ring man and an auctioneer who don't work well together may mis-communicate information, and this could result in lost profits. Even worse, if the auctioneer does not get along with your ring men, the atmosphere may become so tense that no one will want to return for the next sale. So don't just let the auctioneer choose the ring staff – insist on it!

Other Personnel

An auctioneer once said that for every ten seconds he has to wait for an animal to enter the ring, he loses $1000 in sales. But you'll need a lot of help to keep things rolling along efficiently. Your sales manager or your auctioneer may be able to line people up, but in any event, you need to make sure they're available for you on sale day.

Cowboys

You're going to need cowboys who can help get the animals in and out of the ring, and loaded onto trucks at the end of the day. How many cowboys? That will depend on the number of animals, the number and size of the pens, how many animals you can line up at one time, and the types of animals (for example, you'll need more if you need to separate cow- calf pairs). It's best to find cowboys who are used to working in the local sale barns and who know how to handle cattle (particularly registered cattle).

Professional Fitters and Groomers

To get the highest prices, your cattle need to be clean, well-fed, and well-groomed. For all practical purposes, your cattle are going to a beauty pageant, and they need a beauty stylist to help them look their best! Be sure the cattle are properly groomed and fitted for public presentation a few days before the sale.

Gate Pullers

Your cowboys will have enough to do without worrying about opening and closing the gates to the auction ring. Have someone stationed at each gate just for that purpose.

Ticket Writer

If the sale is going well, animals will be selling at a very fast pace. Neither the auctioneer nor the sales manager will have the time to write the tickets (and you wouldn't want them distracted by this, anyway), so have at least one person who can sit with the auctioneer and write sales tickets. It's best to have your auctioneer choose your ticket writer, since auctioneers can be so hard to understand.

Clerks

Be sure to have clerks on hand to register bidders, take payments, fill out bill-of-sale forms, and the like. If you have the clerks handle money, be sure to have that process supervised by someone you trust.

General Helpers

In addition to the people I've already mentioned, you'll want a few people on hand to help out wherever they're needed. These are the people that will cook, set up tables and chairs, pick up the trash, and do all those other jobs that you're not going to want to deal with. Better yet, hire a caterer if you can afford it. It might cost a little more, but it will buy you some extra freedom on the day of the sale.

Veterinarian

It's probably not necessary to have a veterinarian on the premises on the day of the sale (though it could be helpful in case of an injury or a question about an animal's health). Still, you will want to consult with your veterinarian in advance of the sale to make sure each animal has the necessary health certificates before the sale and don't forget to ask him if the health papers may require a redirect. The veterinarian can also confirm pregnancy status for any bred cows you are selling.

Professional Haulers

It's a good idea to have professional haulers lined up on the day of the sale. While many buyers will bring trailers, some will not. And the availability of a hauler is a terrific selling point for someone who came just to watch.

Insurers

You might also want to have an insurance agent available on the day of the sale. Buyers may wish to insure their stock at least until the animals get to their new ranch safely. If you are selling any animals on consignment, insurance is a must for your own protection (though you may want the seller to provide the insurance at his own expense).

You may feel, about now, as though you are hiring too many people. However, as you will see from the next chapter, there's plenty of work to spread around. Once you've got your "cast of thousands" lined up, it's time to start working on all the other details.

Here are a few items to jog your memory when working with a sales manager.

Scheduling for and understanding who will take photos of sale cattle that are worthy of being photographed for advertising and catalog purposes.

A good sales manager will help producer plan an advertising budget and schedule an effective advertising campaign with the publications agreed upon with the customer to be used for promotion of the sale.

The sales manager should facilitate getting all the materials and photos in to these publications by each of their deadlines.

If needed, the sales manager should solicit bids for the production of the catalog, accept a bid for the catalog, and produce, layout, design, print and mail catalog with help from person or firm submitting winning bid. This includes writing all of the footnotes, placing photos, etc. Both sales manager and producer should coordinate on effective mailing list for the distribution of the catalog if needed.

A sales manager should be willing to arrive at sale site up to two days before sale day to help pen the cattle in a way that is most beneficial to the sale and assist in any problems, concerns or situations that may arise.

Sales manager should supply at least a part of the clerking for the sale.

Sales manager and producer both should attempt to market the cattle through the solicitation of buyers through phone calls and personal contacts.

Sales manager should field any phone calls pertaining to the sale cattle and represent potential buyers in the case that they cannot be there in person to bid on cattle.

If needed, sales manager should collect the money on sale day and deposit in a custodial account and pay all of the bills and commissions pertaining to the sale.

Sales manager and producer should decide in advance who will do all the invoicing for those that need to be billed and transfer the registration papers.

The producer should have advance understanding as to the sales manager bonding, etc.

If sales manager does the accounting on the sale he/she should provide a complete financial report of the sale upon closing of the books.

If needed, the sales manager should help or assist producer in finding labor to help with the sale. Some sales managers may have various contacts that work registered cattle sales and can clip the cattle for photos and for the sale itself.

This labor can also be used for anything that needs to be done leading up to the sale, i.e. sorting, penning, washing, etc.

A good sales manager will also handle anything else asked by the customer that is within their power and not mentioned in the list above. Additional expense if any should be disclosed prior to work being done.

Responsibility of costs for the sale: Sales manager should be solely responsible for the costs incurred by sale manager for phone calls, travel, lodging, meals, sale manager staff assistance and their costs, sales supplies as well as any other products and services needed to conduct the business of managing the sale.

All costs pertaining to the production sale are the sole responsibility of the producer and not the sales manager.

Sales manager should have contracts and commission rates available upon request and be available for producer discussion to implement a successful sale.

Chapter Three:
Details, Details

"Obstacles are those frightful things you see when you take your eyes off your goal." *Henry Ford*

There's more to an auction than the personnel, of course. There are a million little details that need to be taken care of. One way to make sure you don't forget anything is to do a mental "run-through" of the sale. That way, you will have the information you'll need to set a budget and begin preparations.

Choosing the Day of the Sale

Time of year: The time of year will depend on the type of livestock you wish to sell, and on local custom. If, for example, you wish to hold a sale of favorite breed of cattle, and you would like to sell a large proportion of cow-calf pairs, then you can calculate a sale date based on that breed's gestation period. Be sure to consult your auctioneer (and sales manager, if you have one) when you determine the sale month.

Day of the week

The day of the week you choose will depend on two main factors: the availability of your auctioneer and sale manager, and the sort of buyers you hope to attract. Rarer breeds, such as the British White, tend to attract hobby farmers who will prefer weekend sales. On the other hand, breeds like Angus and Hereford may attract commercial ranchers who prefer a weekday sale. Again, your auctioneer and sale manager can help you make this determination.

Planning for the weather

You can't predict the weather months in advance, much less plan it. However, you can improve your odds. Avoid dates that are likely to bring severe weather. If you live near the Rocky Mountains, for example, you should not have your sale in mid-March.

In any event, try to prepare for any sort of weather Mother Nature decides to hand out. In other words, unless you live in the desert – and perhaps even then – it's a good idea to arrange for shelter (such as a tent rental) in case of rain.

Deciding Which Animals to Sell

All the costs of a sale are either fixed or based on commission. That means the more money each animal brings, the higher your profits will be. In addition, your sale is a showcase of your ranch, so you want to look your best. Therefore, you should choose your best stock for the sale. Sell your lower-quality stock elsewhere.

Your job, then, is to make an objective assessment of the quality of your stock. If you find it difficult to be objective, your auctioneer or a local livestock judge may be able to help.

All things being equal, the highest prices will go for so-called "three-in-one" packages – that is, a bred cow (or better yet, a heifer) with a calf. Usually the best income producer will be a cow-calf pair where the calf is old enough to split off from the cow in the ring; that is, a pair where the calf is about five to seven months old.

After a three-in-one package, bred cows will go for the next highest price, then bred heifers, open heifers, and finally, bulls.

Consignments

Decide early on whether you would like to include consignments in your sale. Since your costs are fixed, adding consigned animals can increase your total profits. Keep in mind, though, that your per-animal profit for a consigned animal will be lower than for one of your own. Therefore, it is probably not a good idea to substitute your own animal with a consigned animal.

When you are deciding this issue, be sure to think about your reason for having the sale. If one of your main goals is to market your ranch, selling animals from other ranches may (or may not) have an adverse effect on that goal.

Setting the Terms of Your Sale

As with everything else, your auctioneer and sales manager can help you determine the terms of sale. Here are some of the things you'll want to think about:

Reserve

What happens if somebody bids $50 for your best heifer, and no one else bids? Nothing bad, if you have a reserve, your auctioneer and ring men have a good working relationship and keep things moving at a lively pace.

Resist the temptation, though, to overestimate the value of your stock. For example, don't base a reserve on how much you paid for, or put into, a particular animal. Bidders won't know or care what you paid, and if you are holding the sale in a depressed economy, you'll have to lower your expectations accordingly. Watch market prices, attend other sales, and listen to the advice of your auctioneer.

Bills of sale. Your auctioneer or sales manager may have a standard bill-of-sale form. It's a good idea to review the form to make sure it's satisfactory. If you're not happy with the form, check around for an alternative (try your breed organization, for example). Before you put a lot of effort into fiddling with bill-of-sale forms, though, remember that someone already paid a lawyer a lot of money to draft the forms you've got available, and there's at least a 50% chance that it was drafted in your favor.

Guarantees. Think carefully about what sorts of guarantees you want to offer your buyers. Certainly, you want to guarantee that each animal is healthy at the time of sale. If you're offering an animal as a bred cow, you'll want to guarantee that she is pregnant at the time of sale. But do you really want to guarantee the birth of a live, healthy calf? If you're not sure what sort of guarantees to offer, a good guideline is to offer the guarantees customary for your breed, plus a little more.

Load-out procedures. When you hire the cowboys and other sales staff, make it clear that they will be expected to stay for a few hours after the end of the sale to help load the animals. Since your profits depend in part on keeping things running efficiently, make it clear to bidders that you will not permit loadouts until the end of the sale. That way, your cowboys will not be diverted from the sale itself.

Health Certificates. Here is where your veterinarian can be worth her or his weight in gold. Let your veterinarian advise you on what health certificates are required not only in your state, but in nearby states that are likely to attract buyers. If possible, have the certificates in order before the sale (or at least be in a position to provide them at the time of sale). Be careful not to do this too early, though, since many health certificates expire after a certain number of days.

Food and Drink. A livestock sale can be as basic, or as luxurious, as you want. But since you're putting so much time, effort, and money into the event, it would be nice to offer people something besides cattle and dusty cowboys. Think about serving food and drinks. If you want to make it a fancier event, you can have a reception for registered bidders the night before. Or you can keep it simple and just serve hot dogs and chips on the day of the sale.

As for drinks, you can serve bottled water, soft drinks, beer, or anything else you'd like. If you want to serve alcohol, you may want to close the bar during the sale itself to keep your guests focused on the sale. Be sure, too, to check your local laws to make sure there are no restrictions on serving alcohol.

Of course, you don't have to serve food at all. At the very least, though, offer non- alcoholic drinks, particularly if the weather is warm. This will help keep everyone in good spirits as the afternoon wears on.

Whatever you decide to offer, keep it simple, and hire someone to handle cooking and clean-up. You won't feel like picking up trash when it's all over.

Logistics and Equipment. While you're planning the sale, take a walk around your property and look at it objectively. Where will people park? Where will buyers load cattle? How will the pens be set up, and how will you move your animals from place to place? Will you need to rent portable pens? Where will people sit? Will you need to rent tents, tables, or chairs? If it rains, can you set things up so that people can walk on grass, rather than slogging through the mud? Do you have electricity available at the sale site so that you can hook up a sound system?

Printing and Advertising. Even free champagne and a candlelight dinner won't help your sale if nobody knows about it. Advertising your sale is essential. You'll want to have three types of advertising. First, you'll need to print a sale catalog, preferably with photographs of at least some of your animals. Second, you will need to purchase advertising in market bulletins, trade publications, and on the Internet. Finally, you'll need to purchase advertising to announce the results of your sale.

Each type of advertising should be as professional-looking as you can afford to make it. This is particularly true of the catalog, which some buyers and breeders will keep for future reference.

Estimating the Budget. Now that you've run through your ideal sale, you know what personnel you want to hire, and when you'd like to have the sale. You have a good idea of the stock you'd like to sell -- and on what terms -- and you know what sort of extras you'll want to provide your guests. It's going to be a great sale!

Now, though, it's time to face reality.

How much is your dream sale going to cost? As with everything else in life, it will probably cost more than you expect. How much more depends on how carefully you plan your budget. Don't skimp on this step. Make a list of everything you intend to provide, and assign a cost. Don't just guess. Instead, really research the costs. If you're going to hire a sales manager, ask him to provide this information. The more realistic you are about your expectations, the more power you'll have to maximize your profits. After all, that's what this sale is all about.

Once you're satisfied that you've accurately determined your probable costs, estimate how much money you expect your cattle to bring. Will you get the kind of return you want? If not, can you reduce the costs without affecting the quality of the sale?

Once you are happy with the probable financial outcome of the sale, it's time to start preparing for the sale.

Chapter Four
Preparing for the Sale

"There are no shortcuts to any place worth going."
Beverly Sills

You've done your homework, and now it's time for action. There are a number of steps you can take to increase your chances of a successful sale. Your job starts many months before the sale.

Six months Before the Sale

Care of your Cattle. In a very real way, the sale is a beauty pageant for your livestock. The better your animals look, the higher the sale price will be. Fat, clean animals bring more money than thin filthy ones. Therefore, take every opportunity to make each animal look its very best. Make sure your cattle are well-fed, parasite-free, washed, and groomed. If your livestock will be coming off pasture, bring them in a week or two before the sale and begin feeding grain so they will not have the green scours at the sale. If this can't be avoided, be sure to list your sale as "off the grass" in all your marketing materials. If you want the groomers to trim the cattle, have them do this a week or two in advance so the trimming won't look choppy. If any of your animals are halter-broke, take advantage of that, and be prepared to present them in hand at the sale.

To prevent any last-minute trouble, this is also a good time to make sure that each animal is properly tagged (or tattooed) and registered. If you haven't done so already, create a file for each animal consisting of a photograph, immunization and pertinent veterinary records, tag and registration certificate, and pedigree.

Five Months Before the Sale

Preparation and Distribution of the Catalog.

Several months in advance of the sale, you will need to prepare the catalog. If you intend to include photographs of your stock, make sure you use professional-looking photographs that really show off the quality of your animals. A picture of a cow grazing in a pasture will not impress anyone. A picture of the same cow as she is presented with a breeding stock award will be much more useful. If you need to, hire someone to help you take photographs, and take the time to get each animal into a show-like stance. In addition to photographs, you may want to include a pedigree for each animal.

As a convenience to buyers coming from out of town, you might also include general information such as directions and local hotels. Also include the terms of the sale, the preview times and location, and any other information you think your buyers may need.

Be sure to leave yourself plenty of time to get the catalog created, printed, and distributed. The original should be submitted to the printer at least three to four months in advance of the sale, so you will have time to review the proofs and correct any errors. You'll need to know how many copies to print, so before you send the catalog to the printer, prepare a mailing list.

You can do this by using your business and personal contacts, breed directories, and trade magazines. You may also want to print copies that you can leave at local feed stores or other strategic locations.

Mail the catalogs at least one month in advance of the sale. Keep some extras so that you can respond to requests.

Four Months Before the Sale

Advertising. Although your catalog is the most expensive piece of advertising for the sale, it's not the only one. You'll also need to buy advertising space in appropriate publications.

What is an "appropriate" publication? That depends on the breed. For more common breeds like Angus or Herefords, you may only need to advertise locally (unless you have exceptional seed stock). For rarer breeds, though, national advertising may be in order. Always keep in mind that any advertising that sells one more animal is usually profitable.

In addition to advertising in publications, you may want to prepare flyers or brochures that you can distribute as needed. You may also want to consider Internet advertising, particularly with your breed's organization website.

Internet advertising can be very effective, since it is easily accessible and often inexpensive or even free.

Another source of free advertising is the press release. A well-written press release, submitted to your breed or trade publication, has a reasonably good chance of being published. There are plenty of Internet sites that will tell you how to write a good press release.

Finally, arrange in advance to advertise the results of the sale. If it goes as planned, you'll appreciate the chance to brag!

One Month Before the Sale

Coordinating the Logistics. As the sale date approaches, start planning the smaller details with your auctioneer. Decide whether to use bidder numbers or names; make sure you have all the necessary forms in sufficient numbers; hire any personnel that have not been hired already, and reserve any rental equipment you'll need. Be sure, when you reserve the rental equipment that you arrange for pick-up after the sale. This is also a good time to finalize settlement and load-out procedures.

One Week Before the Sale

Final Details. A few days before the sale, confirm that your staff knows where to be and when. You should also confirm food arrangements at this time. Set up the equipment and temporary facilities, and set up your load- out area. Be sure to plan for separating cow-calf pairs before or after the sale, if necessary. Prepare a supplemental sale sheet for any cattle you decided to sell after your catalog went to the printer.

This is also the time for you and your auctioneer to determine the final sale order. A day or two before the sale let your auctioneer look over the animals you will be selling. Based on the quality and types of animals, he can advise you as to the final order.

As the sale approaches, remind yourself of everything you've accomplished: You've hired good people, planned all the details, prepared your stock and your farm, and done all the other footwork required to put on a successful sale , there's no reason to think your sale won't go well. There's only one thing more you can do – get a good night's sleep before the sale!

Chapter Five
The Day of the Sale

"The problem is not that there are problems. The problem is expecting otherwise and thinking that having problems is a problem."
Theodore Rubin

It's no coincidence that this is the shortest chapter in the book. If you've planned carefully, you should have little to do on the day of the sale except eat, socialize, and enjoy the day.

Yes, you may be needed for last-minute problem solving, but your main task on sale day -- unless you're acting as your own sales manager – is to let each person do his (or her) job.

After the Sale

Be sure that no staff members leave until all the cattle have been loaded out. At that time, settle up with all personnel as agreed in advance. Make sure that after-sale tasks have been done as planned, such as publication of the results and pick-up of the equipment. If you have planned the event carefully, you should have little else to do except count your money.

Conclusion

"Don't judge each day by the harvest you reap but by the seeds you plant." Robert Louis Stephenson

After your sale, leave time for reflection. Ask yourself what worked, and what didn't. Think about what you want to do differently next time you hold a sale.

Remember, too, that the success of your sale cannot be measured just_ from accounting spreadsheets. Whether you make a fortune from your first cattle sale, or next to nothing, you're bound to gain experience that will make you a savvier rancher. In fact, the more that goes wrong, the more experience you will probably have gained! And in nearly every case, you will have created valuable goodwill for your ranch and for your breed that will increase your profits many years into the future.

About the Author

"I still find each day too short for all the thoughts I want to think, all the walks I want to take, all the books I want to read, and all the friends I want to see." John Burroughs

Morris Halliburton was born in Texas in 1931, and has been around cattle ever since. He and his family operate a small ranch near Bells, Texas, where they have raised rare British White Cattle since 1989. Mr. Halliburton is prominent in the British White community, and beginning in 1994 he served as Executive Secretary of the British White Cattle Association of America for many years.

Mr. Halliburton has been conducting on-farm sales since 1984. He readily admits that he was "green as a gourd" when he held his first sale. However, thirty plus years of experience since then has provided him with insight not often found among small ranchers.

Morris Halliburton
Halliburton Farms
200 Halliburton Drive
Bells, TX 75

www.ingramcontent.com/pod-product-compliance
Lightning Source LLC
Chambersburg PA
CBHW071251280526
45788CB00004B/1664